This book belongs to:

_____

How to use this Prayer Journal

This is a 60-day prayer journal and can be utilized to explore God's word surrounding different aspects of your life.

How to enjoy the book, Step by Step:

- You will find a list of subjects and corresponding Bible verses on the next page (page 3).

- Each day, select a verse.

- Place a check mark in the circle next to the verse you select indicating that you have completed your studies of the verse

- You will find a space at the top of each day's page to write in the verse that you selected for that day.

- Follow the prompts provided.

STRESS

- Psalm 46:1-3
- Philippians 4:6
- John 14:27
- Psalm 94:19
- Luke 12:25-26
- John 14:27
- Joshua 1:9

FEAR

- Luke 12:22-26
- Psalm 55:22
- Deuteronomy 31:6
- Psalm 46:1
- Psalm 118:6-7
- Psalm 34:4
- Psalm 56:3

HEALTH

- Proverbs 17:22
- Jeremiah 33:6
- Proverbs 16:24
- Proverbs 3:7-8
- Jeremiah 17:14
- Exodus 23:25
- Isaiah 41:10

STRENGTH

- Philippians 4:13
- Isaiah 40:29
- Psalm 119:28
- Ephesians 6:10
- Isaiah 40:31
- Psalm 46:1
- Isaiah 41:10

FINANCES

- Hebrews 13:5
- Matthew 6:21
- Psalm 37:16-17
- Proverbs 13:11
- Matthew 19:21
- Matthew 6:24
- 1 Timothy 6:10

STRUGGLES

- Isaiah 41:13
- 1 Peter 5:7
- James 1:2-4
- Proverbs 3:5-6
- Proverbs 12:25
- Romans 8:28
- James 1:12

PROTECTION

- Psalm 138:7
- Deuteronomy 31:6
- Psalm 20:1
- Psalm 34:19
- Psalm 51:1
- Psalm 140:4

FAITH

- Hebrews 11:1
- Matthew 21:22
- Romans 10:17
- Mark 11:22-24
- Luke 1:37
- 1 Corinthians 2:5

BE THANKFUL

- 1 Chronicles 16:34
- Colossians 3:17
- Colossians 4:2
- Philippians 4:6
- Psalm 28:7
- Psalm 106:1

Today's Date:_____

Let God speak to you through his Word. Select a scripture from Page 3.

Scripture selected:_____

Write down the scripture:

Study the scripture, then pray and answer the following.

Write down how you're feeling about the topic of the scripture:

_____

_____

_____

_____

What's your prayer to God surrounding the scripture?

_____

_____

_____

_____

Other Prayer Requests:

_____   _____

_____   _____

_____   _____

_____   _____

Answered Prayer Requests:

_____   _____

_____   _____

_____   _____

_____   _____

Today I am most thankful for:

_____

_____

_____

_____

Today's Date:_____

Let God speak to you through his Word. Select a scripture from Page 3.

Scripture selected:_____

Write down the scripture:

Study the scripture, then pray and answer the following.

⁘⁘⁘⁘⁘⁘⁘⁘⁘

Write down how you're feeling about the topic of the scripture:

_____

_____

_____

_____

⁘⁘⁘⁘⁘⁘⁘⁘⁘

What's your prayer to God surrounding the scripture?

_____

_____

_____

_____

Other Prayer Requests:

_____   _____

_____   _____

_____   _____

_____   _____

Answered Prayer Requests:

_____   _____

_____   _____

_____   _____

_____   _____

Today I am most thankful for:

_____

_____

_____

_____

Today's Date:_____

Let God speak to you through his Word. Select a scripture from Page 3.

Scripture selected:_____

Write down the scripture:

Study the scripture, then pray and answer the following.

⌒⌒⌒⌒·⌒⌒⌒·⌒⌒⌒·⌒⌒⌒·

Write down how you're feeling about the topic of the scripture:

_____

_____

_____

_____

⌒⌒⌒⌒·⌒⌒⌒·⌒⌒⌒·⌒⌒⌒·

What's your prayer to God surrounding the scripture?

_____

_____

_____

_____

Other Prayer Requests:

_____   _____

_____   _____

_____   _____

_____   _____

Answered Prayer Requests:

_____   _____

_____   _____

_____   _____

_____   _____

Today I am most thankful for:

_____

_____

_____

_____

Today's Date:_____

Let God speak to you through his Word. Select a scripture from Page 3.

Scripture selected:_____

Write down the scripture:

Study the scripture, then pray and answer the following.

〜 〜 〜 〜 〜 〜 〜 〜

Write down how you're feeling about the topic of the scripture:

_____

_____

_____

_____

〜 〜 〜 〜 〜 〜 〜 〜

What's your prayer to God surrounding the scripture?

_____

_____

_____

_____

Other Prayer Requests:

_____   _____

_____   _____

_____   _____

_____   _____

Answered Prayer Requests:

_____   _____

_____   _____

_____   _____

_____   _____

Today I am most thankful for:

_____

_____

_____

_____

Today's Date:_____

Let God speak to you through his Word. Select a scripture from Page 3.

Scripture selected:_____

Write down the scripture:

Study the scripture, then pray and answer the following.

Write down how you're feeling about the topic of the scripture:

_____

_____

_____

_____

What's your prayer to God surrounding the scripture?

_____

_____

_____

_____

Other Prayer Requests:

_____   _____

_____   _____

_____   _____

_____   _____

Answered Prayer Requests:

_____   _____

_____   _____

_____   _____

_____   _____

Today I am most thankful for:

_____

_____

_____

_____

Today's Date:_____

Let God speak to you through his Word. Select a scripture from Page 3.

Scripture selected:_____

Write down the scripture:

Study the scripture, then pray and answer the following.

Write down how you're feeling about the topic of the scripture:

_____

_____

_____

_____

What's your prayer to God surrounding the scripture?

_____

_____

_____

_____

Other Prayer Requests:

_____ _____

_____ _____

_____ _____

_____ _____

Answered Prayer Requests:

_____ _____

_____ _____

_____ _____

_____ _____

Today I am most thankful for:

_____

_____

_____

_____

Today's Date:_____

Let God speak to you through his Word. Select a scripture from Page 3.

Scripture selected:_____

Write down the scripture:

Study the scripture, then pray and answer the following.

Write down how you're feeling about the topic of the scripture:

_____

_____

_____

_____

What's your prayer to God surrounding the scripture?

_____

_____

_____

_____

Other Prayer Requests:

_____   _____

_____   _____

_____   _____

_____   _____

Answered Prayer Requests:

_____   _____

_____   _____

_____   _____

_____   _____

Today I am most thankful for:

_____

_____

_____

_____

Today's Date:_____

Let God speak to you through his Word. Select a scripture from Page 3.

Scripture selected:_____

Write down the scripture:

Study the scripture, then pray and answer the following.

⤫⤫⤫⤫⤫⤫⤫⤫⤫⤫

Write down how you're feeling about the topic of the scripture:

_____

_____

_____

_____

⤫⤫⤫⤫⤫⤫⤫⤫⤫⤫

What's your prayer to God surrounding the scripture?

_____

_____

_____

_____

Other Prayer Requests:

_____   _____

_____   _____

_____   _____

_____   _____

Answered Prayer Requests:

_____   _____

_____   _____

_____   _____

_____   _____

Today I am most thankful for:

_____

_____

_____

_____

Today's Date:_____

Let God speak to you through his Word. Select a scripture from Page 3.

Scripture selected:_____

Write down the scripture:

Study the scripture, then pray and answer the following.

Write down how you're feeling about the topic of the scripture:

_____

_____

_____

_____

What's your prayer to God surrounding the scripture?

_____

_____

_____

_____

Other Prayer Requests:

_____   _____

_____   _____

_____   _____

_____   _____

Answered Prayer Requests:

_____   _____

_____   _____

_____   _____

_____   _____

Today I am most thankful for:

_____

_____

_____

_____

Today's Date:_____

Let God speak to you through his Word. Select a scripture from Page 3.

Scripture selected:_____

Write down the scripture:

Study the scripture, then pray and answer the following.

Write down how you're feeling about the topic of the scripture:

_____

_____

_____

_____

What's your prayer to God surrounding the scripture?

_____

_____

_____

_____

Other Prayer Requests:

_____   _____

_____   _____

_____   _____

_____   _____

Answered Prayer Requests:

_____   _____

_____   _____

_____   _____

_____   _____

Today I am most thankful for:

_____

_____

_____

_____

Today's Date:_____

Let God speak to you through his Word. Select a scripture from Page 3.

Scripture selected:_____

Write down the scripture:

Study the scripture, then pray and answer the following.

Write down how you're feeling about the topic of the scripture:

_____

_____

_____

_____

What's your prayer to God surrounding the scripture?

_____

_____

_____

_____

Other Prayer Requests:

_____   _____

_____   _____

_____   _____

_____   _____

Answered Prayer Requests:

_____   _____

_____   _____

_____   _____

_____   _____

Today I am most thankful for:

_____

_____

_____

_____

Today's Date:_____

Let God speak to you through his Word. Select a scripture from Page 3.

Scripture selected:_____

Write down the scripture:

Study the scripture, then pray and answer the following.

Write down how you're feeling about the topic of the scripture:

_____

_____

_____

_____

What's your prayer to God surrounding the scripture?

_____

_____

_____

_____

Other Prayer Requests:

_____   _____

_____   _____

_____   _____

_____   _____

Answered Prayer Requests:

_____   _____

_____   _____

_____   _____

_____   _____

Today I am most thankful for:

_____

_____

_____

_____

Today's Date:_____

Let God speak to you through his Word. Select a scripture from Page 3.

Scripture selected:_____

Write down the scripture:

Study the scripture, then pray and answer the following.

Write down how you're feeling about the topic of the scripture:

_____

_____

_____

_____

What's your prayer to God surrounding the scripture?

_____

_____

_____

_____

Other Prayer Requests:

_____   _____

_____   _____

_____   _____

_____   _____

Answered Prayer Requests:

_____   _____

_____   _____

_____   _____

_____   _____

Today I am most thankful for:

_____

_____

_____

_____

Today's Date:_____

Let God speak to you through his Word. Select a scripture from Page 3.

Scripture selected:_____

Write down the scripture:

Study the scripture, then pray and answer the following.

Write down how you're feeling about the topic of the scripture:

_____

_____

_____

_____

What's your prayer to God surrounding the scripture?

_____

_____

_____

_____

Other Prayer Requests:

_____   _____

_____   _____

_____   _____

_____   _____

Answered Prayer Requests:

_____   _____

_____   _____

_____   _____

_____   _____

Today I am most thankful for:

_____

_____

_____

_____

Today's Date:_____

Let God speak to you through his Word. Select a scripture from Page 3.

Scripture selected:_____

Write down the scripture:

Study the scripture, then pray and answer the following.

Write down how you're feeling about the topic of the scripture:

_____

_____

_____

_____

What's your prayer to God surrounding the scripture?

_____

_____

_____

_____

Other Prayer Requests:

_____   _____

_____   _____

_____   _____

_____   _____

Answered Prayer Requests:

_____   _____

_____   _____

_____   _____

_____   _____

Today I am most thankful for:

_____

_____

_____

_____

Today's Date:_____

Let God speak to you through his Word. Select a scripture from Page 3.

Scripture selected:_____

Write down the scripture:

Study the scripture, then pray and answer the following.

⌘⌘⌘⌘⌘⌘⌘⌘

Write down how you're feeling about the topic of the scripture:

_____

_____

_____

_____

⌘⌘⌘⌘⌘⌘⌘⌘

What's your prayer to God surrounding the scripture?

_____

_____

_____

_____

Other Prayer Requests:

_____   _____

_____   _____

_____   _____

_____   _____

Answered Prayer Requests:

_____   _____

_____   _____

_____   _____

_____   _____

Today I am most thankful for:

_____

_____

_____

_____

Today's Date:_____

Let God speak to you through his Word. Select a scripture from Page 3.

Scripture selected:_____

Write down the scripture:

Study the scripture, then pray and answer the following.

Write down how you're feeling about the topic of the scripture:

_____

_____

_____

_____

What's your prayer to God surrounding the scripture?

_____

_____

_____

_____

Other Prayer Requests:

_____   _____

_____   _____

_____   _____

_____   _____

Answered Prayer Requests:

_____   _____

_____   _____

_____   _____

_____   _____

Today I am most thankful for:

_____

_____

_____

_____

Today's Date:_____

Let God speak to you through his Word. Select a scripture from Page 3.

Scripture selected:_____

Write down the scripture:

Study the scripture, then pray and answer the following.

Write down how you're feeling about the topic of the scripture:

_____

_____

_____

_____

What's your prayer to God surrounding the scripture?

_____

_____

_____

_____

Other Prayer Requests:

_____   _____

_____   _____

_____   _____

_____   _____

Answered Prayer Requests:

_____   _____

_____   _____

_____   _____

_____   _____

Today I am most thankful for:

_____

_____

_____

_____

Today's Date:_____

Let God speak to you through his Word. Select a scripture from Page 3.

Scripture selected:_____

Write down the scripture:

Study the scripture, then pray and answer the following.

Write down how you're feeling about the topic of the scripture:

_____

_____

_____

_____

What's your prayer to God surrounding the scripture?

_____

_____

_____

_____

Other Prayer Requests:

_____ _____
_____ _____
_____ _____
_____ _____

Answered Prayer Requests:

_____ _____
_____ _____
_____ _____
_____ _____

Today I am most thankful for:

_____
_____
_____
_____

Today's Date:_____

Let God speak to you through his Word. Select a scripture from Page 3.

Scripture selected:_____

Write down the scripture:

Study the scripture, then pray and answer the following.

Write down how you're feeling about the topic of the scripture:

_____

_____

_____

_____

What's your prayer to God surrounding the scripture?

_____

_____

_____

_____

Other Prayer Requests:

_____   _____

_____   _____

_____   _____

_____   _____

Answered Prayer Requests:

_____   _____

_____   _____

_____   _____

_____   _____

Today I am most thankful for:

_____

_____

_____

_____

Today's Date:_____

Let God speak to you through his Word. Select a scripture from Page 3.

Scripture selected:_____

Write down the scripture:

Study the scripture, then pray and answer the following.

Write down how you're feeling about the topic of the scripture:

_____

_____

_____

_____

What's your prayer to God surrounding the scripture?

_____

_____

_____

_____

Other Prayer Requests:

_____   _____

_____   _____

_____   _____

_____   _____

Answered Prayer Requests:

_____   _____

_____   _____

_____   _____

_____   _____

Today I am most thankful for:

_____

_____

_____

_____

Today's Date:_____

Let God speak to you through his Word. Select a scripture from Page 3.

Scripture selected:_____

Write down the scripture:

Study the scripture, then pray and answer the following.

Write down how you're feeling about the topic of the scripture:

_____

_____

_____

_____

What's your prayer to God surrounding the scripture?

_____

_____

_____

_____

Other Prayer Requests:

_____   _____

_____   _____

_____   _____

_____   _____

Answered Prayer Requests:

_____   _____

_____   _____

_____   _____

_____   _____

Today I am most thankful for:

_____

_____

_____

_____

Today's Date:_____

Let God speak to you through his Word. Select a scripture from Page 3.

Scripture selected:_____

Write down the scripture:

Study the scripture, then pray and answer the following.

Write down how you're feeling about the topic of the scripture:

_____

_____

_____

_____

What's your prayer to God surrounding the scripture?

_____

_____

_____

_____

Other Prayer Requests:

_____   _____

_____   _____

_____   _____

_____   _____

Answered Prayer Requests:

_____   _____

_____   _____

_____   _____

_____   _____

Today I am most thankful for:

_____

_____

_____

_____

Today's Date:_____

Let God speak to you through his Word. Select a scripture from Page 3.

Scripture selected:_____

Write down the scripture:

Study the scripture, then pray and answer the following.

Write down how you're feeling about the topic of the scripture:

_____

_____

_____

_____

What's your prayer to God surrounding the scripture?

_____

_____

_____

_____

Other Prayer Requests:

_____   _____

_____   _____

_____   _____

_____   _____

Answered Prayer Requests:

_____   _____

_____   _____

_____   _____

_____   _____

Today I am most thankful for:

_____

_____

_____

_____

Today's Date:_____

Let God speak to you through his Word. Select a scripture from Page 3.

Scripture selected:_____

Write down the scripture:

Study the scripture, then pray and answer the following.

Write down how you're feeling about the topic of the scripture:

_____

_____

_____

_____

What's your prayer to God surrounding the scripture?

_____

_____

_____

_____

Other Prayer Requests:

_____   _____

_____   _____

_____   _____

_____   _____

Answered Prayer Requests:

_____   _____

_____   _____

_____   _____

_____   _____

Today I am most thankful for:

_____

_____

_____

_____

Today's Date:_____

Let God speak to you through his Word. Select a scripture from Page 3.

Scripture selected:_____

Write down the scripture:

Study the scripture, then pray and answer the following.

Write down how you're feeling about the topic of the scripture:

_____

_____

_____

_____

What's your prayer to God surrounding the scripture?

_____

_____

_____

_____

Other Prayer Requests:

_____   _____

_____   _____

_____   _____

_____   _____

Answered Prayer Requests:

_____   _____

_____   _____

_____   _____

_____   _____

Today I am most thankful for:

_____

_____

_____

_____

Today's Date:_____

Let God speak to you through his Word. Select a scripture from Page 3.

Scripture selected:_____

Write down the scripture:

Study the scripture, then pray and answer the following.

Write down how you're feeling about the topic of the scripture:

_____

_____

_____

_____

What's your prayer to God surrounding the scripture?

_____

_____

_____

_____

Other Prayer Requests:

_____   _____

_____   _____

_____   _____

_____   _____

Answered Prayer Requests:

_____   _____

_____   _____

_____   _____

_____   _____

Today I am most thankful for:

_____

_____

_____

_____

Today's Date:_____

Let God speak to you through his Word. Select a scripture from Page 3.

Scripture selected:_____

Write down the scripture:

Study the scripture, then pray and answer the following.

Write down how you're feeling about the topic of the scripture:

_____

_____

_____

_____

What's your prayer to God surrounding the scripture?

_____

_____

_____

_____

Other Prayer Requests:

_____   _____

_____   _____

_____   _____

_____   _____

Answered Prayer Requests:

_____   _____

_____   _____

_____   _____

_____   _____

Today I am most thankful for:

_____

_____

_____

_____

Today's Date:_____

Let God speak to you through his Word. Select a scripture from Page 3.

Scripture selected:_____

Write down the scripture:

Study the scripture, then pray and answer the following.

Write down how you're feeling about the topic of the scripture:

_____

_____

_____

_____

What's your prayer to God surrounding the scripture?

_____

_____

_____

_____

Other Prayer Requests:

_____   _____

_____   _____

_____   _____

_____   _____

Answered Prayer Requests:

_____   _____

_____   _____

_____   _____

_____   _____

Today I am most thankful for:

_____

_____

_____

_____

Today's Date:_____

Let God speak to you through his Word. Select a scripture from Page 3.

Scripture selected:_____

Write down the scripture:

Study the scripture, then pray and answer the following.

Write down how you're feeling about the topic of the scripture:

_____

_____

_____

_____

What's your prayer to God surrounding the scripture?

_____

_____

_____

_____

Other Prayer Requests:

_____ _____

_____ _____

_____ _____

_____ _____

Answered Prayer Requests:

_____ _____

_____ _____

_____ _____

_____ _____

Today I am most thankful for:

_____

_____

_____

_____

Today's Date:_____

Let God speak to you through his Word. Select a scripture from Page 3.

Scripture selected:_____

Write down the scripture:

Study the scripture, then pray and answer the following.

Write down how you're feeling about the topic of the scripture:

_____

_____

_____

_____

What's your prayer to God surrounding the scripture?

_____

_____

_____

_____

Other Prayer Requests:

_____   _____

_____   _____

_____   _____

_____   _____

Answered Prayer Requests:

_____   _____

_____   _____

_____   _____

_____   _____

Today I am most thankful for:

_____

_____

_____

_____

Today's Date:_____

Let God speak to you through his Word. Select a scripture from Page 3.

Scripture selected:_____

Write down the scripture:

Study the scripture, then pray and answer the following.

Write down how you're feeling about the topic of the scripture:

_____

_____

_____

_____

What's your prayer to God surrounding the scripture?

_____

_____

_____

_____

Other Prayer Requests:

_____   _____

_____   _____

_____   _____

_____   _____

Answered Prayer Requests:

_____   _____

_____   _____

_____   _____

_____   _____

Today I am most thankful for:

_____

_____

_____

_____

Today's Date:_____

Let God speak to you through his Word. Select a scripture from Page 3.

Scripture selected:_____

Write down the scripture:

Study the scripture, then pray and answer the following.

Write down how you're feeling about the topic of the scripture:

_____

_____

_____

_____

What's your prayer to God surrounding the scripture?

_____

_____

_____

_____

Other Prayer Requests:

_____   _____

_____   _____

_____   _____

_____   _____

Answered Prayer Requests:

_____   _____

_____   _____

_____   _____

_____   _____

Today I am most thankful for:

_____

_____

_____

_____

Today's Date:_____

Let God speak to you through his Word. Select a scripture from Page 3.

Scripture selected:_____

Write down the scripture:

Study the scripture, then pray and answer the following.

Write down how you're feeling about the topic of the scripture:

_____

_____

_____

_____

What's your prayer to God surrounding the scripture?

_____

_____

_____

_____

Other Prayer Requests:

_____ _____

_____ _____

_____ _____

_____ _____

Answered Prayer Requests:

_____ _____

_____ _____

_____ _____

_____ _____

Today I am most thankful for:

_____

_____

_____

_____

Today's Date:_____

Let God speak to you through his Word. Select a scripture from Page 3.

Scripture selected:_____

Write down the scripture:

Study the scripture, then pray and answer the following.

Write down how you're feeling about the topic of the scripture:

_____

_____

_____

_____

What's your prayer to God surrounding the scripture?

_____

_____

_____

_____

Other Prayer Requests:

_____   _____

_____   _____

_____   _____

_____   _____

Answered Prayer Requests:

_____   _____

_____   _____

_____   _____

_____   _____

Today I am most thankful for:

_____

_____

_____

_____

Today's Date:_____

Let God speak to you through his Word. Select a scripture from Page 3.

Scripture selected:_____

Write down the scripture:

Study the scripture, then pray and answer the following.

Write down how you're feeling about the topic of the scripture:

_____

_____

_____

_____

What's your prayer to God surrounding the scripture?

_____

_____

_____

_____

Other Prayer Requests:

_____ _____

_____ _____

_____ _____

_____ _____

Answered Prayer Requests:

_____ _____

_____ _____

_____ _____

_____ _____

Today I am most thankful for:

_____

_____

_____

_____

Today's Date:_____

Let God speak to you through his Word. Select a scripture from Page 3.

Scripture selected:_____

Write down the scripture:

Study the scripture, then pray and answer the following.

Write down how you're feeling about the topic of the scripture:

_____

_____

_____

_____

What's your prayer to God surrounding the scripture?

_____

_____

_____

_____

Other Prayer Requests:

_____   _____

_____   _____

_____   _____

_____   _____

Answered Prayer Requests:

_____   _____

_____   _____

_____   _____

_____   _____

Today I am most thankful for:

_____

_____

_____

_____

Today's Date:_____

Let God speak to you through his Word. Select a scripture from Page 3.

Scripture selected:_____

Write down the scripture:

Study the scripture, then pray and answer the following.

Write down how you're feeling about the topic of the scripture:

_____

_____

_____

_____

What's your prayer to God surrounding the scripture?

_____

_____

_____

_____

Other Prayer Requests:

_____   _____

_____   _____

_____   _____

_____   _____

Answered Prayer Requests:

_____   _____

_____   _____

_____   _____

_____   _____

Today I am most thankful for:

_____

_____

_____

_____

Today's Date:_____

Let God speak to you through his Word. Select a scripture from Page 3.

Scripture selected:_____

Write down the scripture:

Study the scripture, then pray and answer the following.

~~~~~~~~~~~~~~~~~~~~~~~~~~~~~~~

Write down how you're feeling about the topic of the scripture:

_____

_____

_____

_____

~~~~~~~~~~~~~~~~~~~~~~~~~~~~~~~

What's your prayer to God surrounding the scripture?

_____

_____

_____

_____

Other Prayer Requests:

_____   _____

_____   _____

_____   _____

_____   _____

Answered Prayer Requests:

_____   _____

_____   _____

_____   _____

_____   _____

Today I am most thankful for:

_____

_____

_____

_____

Today's Date:_____

Let God speak to you through his Word. Select a scripture from Page 3.

Scripture selected:_____

Write down the scripture:

Study the scripture, then pray and answer the following.

⌘ ⌘ · ⌘ ⌘ · ⌘ ⌘ · ⌘ ⌘ ·

Write down how you're feeling about the topic of the scripture:

_____

_____

_____

_____

⌘ ⌘ · ⌘ ⌘ · ⌘ ⌘ · ⌘ ⌘ ·

What's your prayer to God surrounding the scripture?

_____

_____

_____

_____

Other Prayer Requests:

_____   _____

_____   _____

_____   _____

_____   _____

Answered Prayer Requests:

_____   _____

_____   _____

_____   _____

_____   _____

Today I am most thankful for:

_____

_____

_____

_____

Today's Date:_____

Let God speak to you through his Word. Select a scripture from Page 3.

Scripture selected:_____

Write down the scripture:

Study the scripture, then pray and answer the following.

Write down how you're feeling about the topic of the scripture:

_____

_____

_____

_____

What's your prayer to God surrounding the scripture?

_____

_____

_____

_____

Other Prayer Requests:

_____   _____

_____   _____

_____   _____

_____   _____

Answered Prayer Requests:

_____   _____

_____   _____

_____   _____

_____   _____

Today I am most thankful for:

_____

_____

_____

_____

Today's Date:_____

Let God speak to you through his Word. Select a scripture from Page 3.

Scripture selected:_____

Write down the scripture:

Study the scripture, then pray and answer the following.

Write down how you're feeling about the topic of the scripture:

_____

_____

_____

_____

What's your prayer to God surrounding the scripture?

_____

_____

_____

_____

Other Prayer Requests:

_____   _____

_____   _____

_____   _____

_____   _____

Answered Prayer Requests:

_____   _____

_____   _____

_____   _____

_____   _____

Today I am most thankful for:

_____

_____

_____

_____

Today's Date:_____

Let God speak to you through his Word. Select a scripture from Page 3.

Scripture selected:_____

Write down the scripture:

Study the scripture, then pray and answer the following.

Write down how you're feeling about the topic of the scripture:

_____

_____

_____

_____

What's your prayer to God surrounding the scripture?

_____

_____

_____

_____

Other Prayer Requests:

_____   _____

_____   _____

_____   _____

_____   _____

Answered Prayer Requests:

_____   _____

_____   _____

_____   _____

_____   _____

Today I am most thankful for:

_____

_____

_____

_____

Today's Date:_____

Let God speak to you through his Word. Select a scripture from Page 3.

Scripture selected:_____

Write down the scripture:

Study the scripture, then pray and answer the following.

Write down how you're feeling about the topic of the scripture:

_____

_____

_____

_____

What's your prayer to God surrounding the scripture?

_____

_____

_____

_____

Other Prayer Requests:

_____ _____

_____ _____

_____ _____

_____ _____

Answered Prayer Requests:

_____ _____

_____ _____

_____ _____

_____ _____

Today I am most thankful for:

_____

_____

_____

_____

Today's Date:_____

Let God speak to you through his Word. Select a scripture from Page 3.

Scripture selected:_____

Write down the scripture:

Study the scripture, then pray and answer the following.

Write down how you're feeling about the topic of the scripture:

_____

_____

_____

_____

What's your prayer to God surrounding the scripture?

_____

_____

_____

_____

Other Prayer Requests:

_____   _____

_____   _____

_____   _____

_____   _____

Answered Prayer Requests:

_____   _____

_____   _____

_____   _____

_____   _____

Today I am most thankful for:

_____

_____

_____

_____

Today's Date:_____

Let God speak to you through his Word. Select a scripture from Page 3.

Scripture selected:_____

Write down the scripture:

Study the scripture, then pray and answer the following.

Write down how you're feeling about the topic of the scripture:

_____

_____

_____

_____

What's your prayer to God surrounding the scripture?

_____

_____

_____

_____

Other Prayer Requests:

_____   _____

_____   _____

_____   _____

_____   _____

Answered Prayer Requests:

_____   _____

_____   _____

_____   _____

_____   _____

Today I am most thankful for:

_____

_____

_____

_____

Today's Date:_____

Let God speak to you through his Word. Select a scripture from Page 3.

Scripture selected:_____

Write down the scripture:

Study the scripture, then pray and answer the following.

Write down how you're feeling about the topic of the scripture:

_____

_____

_____

_____

What's your prayer to God surrounding the scripture?

_____

_____

_____

_____

Other Prayer Requests:

_____   _____

_____   _____

_____   _____

_____   _____

Answered Prayer Requests:

_____   _____

_____   _____

_____   _____

_____   _____

Today I am most thankful for:

_____

_____

_____

_____

Today's Date:_____

Let God speak to you through his Word. Select a scripture from Page 3.

Scripture selected:_____

Write down the scripture:

Study the scripture, then pray and answer the following.

Write down how you're feeling about the topic of the scripture:

_____

_____

_____

_____

What's your prayer to God surrounding the scripture?

_____

_____

_____

_____

Other Prayer Requests:

_____   _____

_____   _____

_____   _____

_____   _____

Answered Prayer Requests:

_____   _____

_____   _____

_____   _____

_____   _____

Today I am most thankful for:

_____

_____

_____

_____

Today's Date:_____

Let God speak to you through his Word. Select a scripture from Page 3.

Scripture selected:_____

Write down the scripture:

Study the scripture, then pray and answer the following.

Write down how you're feeling about the topic of the scripture:

_____

_____

_____

_____

What's your prayer to God surrounding the scripture?

_____

_____

_____

_____

Other Prayer Requests:

_____   _____

_____   _____

_____   _____

_____   _____

Answered Prayer Requests:

_____   _____

_____   _____

_____   _____

_____   _____

Today I am most thankful for:

_____

_____

_____

_____

Today's Date:_____

Let God speak to you through his Word. Select a scripture from Page 3.

Scripture selected:_____

Write down the scripture:

Study the scripture, then pray and answer the following.

Write down how you're feeling about the topic of the scripture:

_____

_____

_____

_____

What's your prayer to God surrounding the scripture?

_____

_____

_____

_____

Other Prayer Requests:

_____   _____

_____   _____

_____   _____

_____   _____

Answered Prayer Requests:

_____   _____

_____   _____

_____   _____

_____   _____

Today I am most thankful for:

_____

_____

_____

_____

Today's Date:_____

Let God speak to you through his Word. Select a scripture from Page 3.

Scripture selected:_____

Write down the scripture:

Study the scripture, then pray and answer the following.

Write down how you're feeling about the topic of the scripture:

_____

_____

_____

_____

What's your prayer to God surrounding the scripture?

_____

_____

_____

_____

Other Prayer Requests:

_____   _____

_____   _____

_____   _____

_____   _____

Answered Prayer Requests:

_____   _____

_____   _____

_____   _____

_____   _____

Today I am most thankful for:

_____

_____

_____

_____

Today's Date:_____

Let God speak to you through his Word. Select a scripture from Page 3.

Scripture selected:_____

Write down the scripture:

Study the scripture, then pray and answer the following.

Write down how you're feeling about the topic of the scripture:

_____

_____

_____

_____

What's your prayer to God surrounding the scripture?

_____

_____

_____

_____

Other Prayer Requests:

_____   _____

_____   _____

_____   _____

_____   _____

Answered Prayer Requests:

_____   _____

_____   _____

_____   _____

_____   _____

Today I am most thankful for:

_____

_____

_____

_____

Today's Date:_____

Let God speak to you through his Word. Select a scripture from Page 3.

Scripture selected:_____

Write down the scripture:

Study the scripture, then pray and answer the following.

Write down how you're feeling about the topic of the scripture:

_____

_____

_____

_____

What's your prayer to God surrounding the scripture?

_____

_____

_____

_____

Other Prayer Requests:

_____   _____

_____   _____

_____   _____

_____   _____

Answered Prayer Requests:

_____   _____

_____   _____

_____   _____

_____   _____

Today I am most thankful for:

_____

_____

_____

_____

Today's Date:_____

Let God speak to you through his Word. Select a scripture from Page 3.

Scripture selected:_____

Write down the scripture:

Study the scripture, then pray and answer the following.

Write down how you're feeling about the topic of the scripture:

_____

_____

_____

_____

What's your prayer to God surrounding the scripture?

_____

_____

_____

_____

Other Prayer Requests:

_____ _____

_____ _____

_____ _____

_____ _____

Answered Prayer Requests:

_____ _____

_____ _____

_____ _____

_____ _____

Today I am most thankful for:

_____

_____

_____

_____

Today's Date:_____

Let God speak to you through his Word. Select a scripture from Page 3.

Scripture selected:_____

Write down the scripture:

Study the scripture, then pray and answer the following.

Write down how you're feeling about the topic of the scripture:

_____

_____

_____

_____

What's your prayer to God surrounding the scripture?

_____

_____

_____

_____

Other Prayer Requests:

_____   _____

_____   _____

_____   _____

_____   _____

Answered Prayer Requests:

_____   _____

_____   _____

_____   _____

_____   _____

Today I am most thankful for:

_____

_____

_____

_____

Today's Date:_____

Let God speak to you through his Word. Select a scripture from Page 3.

Scripture selected:_____

Write down the scripture:

Study the scripture, then pray and answer the following.

∾ ⌒ ∾ · ∾ ⌒ ∾ · ∾ ⌒ ∾ · ∾ ⌒ ∾ ·

Write down how you're feeling about the topic of the scripture:

_____

_____

_____

_____

∾ ⌒ ∾ · ∾ ⌒ ∾ · ∾ ⌒ ∾ · ∾ ⌒ ∾ ·

What's your prayer to God surrounding the scripture?

_____

_____

_____

_____

Other Prayer Requests:

_____ _____

_____ _____

_____ _____

_____ _____

Answered Prayer Requests:

_____ _____

_____ _____

_____ _____

_____ _____

Today I am most thankful for:

_____

_____

_____

_____

Today's Date:_____

Let God speak to you through his Word. Select a scripture from Page 3.

Scripture selected:_____

Write down the scripture:

Study the scripture, then pray and answer the following.

Write down how you're feeling about the topic of the scripture:

_____

_____

_____

_____

What's your prayer to God surrounding the scripture?

_____

_____

_____

_____

Other Prayer Requests:

_____   _____

_____   _____

_____   _____

_____   _____

Answered Prayer Requests:

_____   _____

_____   _____

_____   _____

_____   _____

Today I am most thankful for:

_____

_____

_____

_____

Today's Date:_____

Let God speak to you through his Word. Select a scripture from Page 3.

Scripture selected:_____

Write down the scripture:

Study the scripture, then pray and answer the following.

Write down how you're feeling about the topic of the scripture:

_____

_____

_____

_____

What's your prayer to God surrounding the scripture?

_____

_____

_____

_____

Other Prayer Requests:

_____   _____

_____   _____

_____   _____

_____   _____

Answered Prayer Requests:

_____   _____

_____   _____

_____   _____

_____   _____

Today I am most thankful for:

_____

_____

_____

_____

Today's Date:_____

Let God speak to you through his Word. Select a scripture from Page 3.

Scripture selected:_____

Write down the scripture:

Study the scripture, then pray and answer the following.

Write down how you're feeling about the topic of the scripture:

_____

_____

_____

_____

What's your prayer to God surrounding the scripture?

_____

_____

_____

_____

Other Prayer Requests:

_____   _____

_____   _____

_____   _____

_____   _____

Answered Prayer Requests:

_____   _____

_____   _____

_____   _____

_____   _____

Today I am most thankful for:

_____

_____

_____

_____

Today's Date:_____

Let God speak to you through his Word. Select a scripture from Page 3.

Scripture selected:_____

Write down the scripture:

Study the scripture, then pray and answer the following.

Write down how you're feeling about the topic of the scripture:

_____

_____

_____

_____

What's your prayer to God surrounding the scripture?

_____

_____

_____

_____

Other Prayer Requests:

_____   _____

_____   _____

_____   _____

_____   _____

Answered Prayer Requests:

_____   _____

_____   _____

_____   _____

_____   _____

Today I am most thankful for:

_____

_____

_____

_____

Made in United States
North Haven, CT
01 February 2023

31961769R00067